What Friends Are For

MEGAN HESS

First published in 2004 by
Piatkus Books Ltd
5 Windmill Street
London W1T 2JA

Website: www.piatkus.co.uk
Email: info@piatkus.co.uk

ISBN 0 7499 2521 3

Text design and setting by
Mark Jonathan Latter

Printed in China by
Everbest Printing Co., Ltd

For Jenni de Weger for being my friend since we were twelve years old and promising to still be there for me when we're both crazy little old ladies.

Acknowledgements

To Alice Davis for making this little book happen and through hundreds of emails becoming my friend.

And to all my friends who have laughed and cried with me over the years. Your friendship has inspired every single page of this book.

Especially Kerrie and Tom. It's nice to know that your brother and sister truly are your best friends.

Getting an honest opinion

Someone to sit with you
in the doctor's waiting room

Girls' night out

Meeting up for a chat

Having someone to phone
in an emergency

Having someone to laugh with

Having someone to cry with

Having someone who listens

Going on holiday

Having a stand-by date

Late night chats

Keeping a secret

Preparing for a date

Supporting you

Inspiring you

Remembering old times

Celebrating the good times

Forgetting the bad times

Being able to be yourself

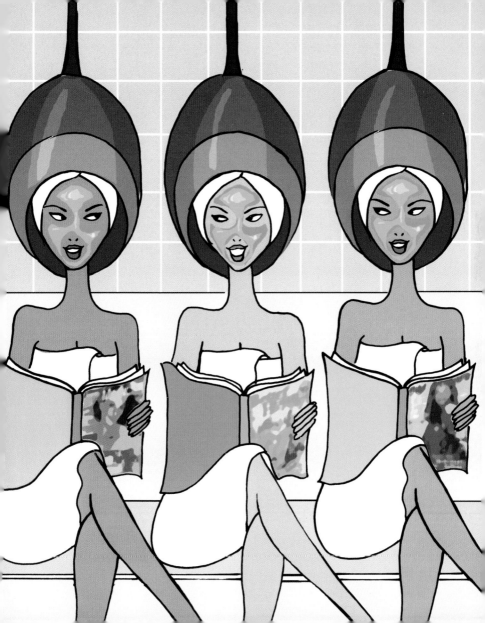

Giving advice

Helping with emergencies

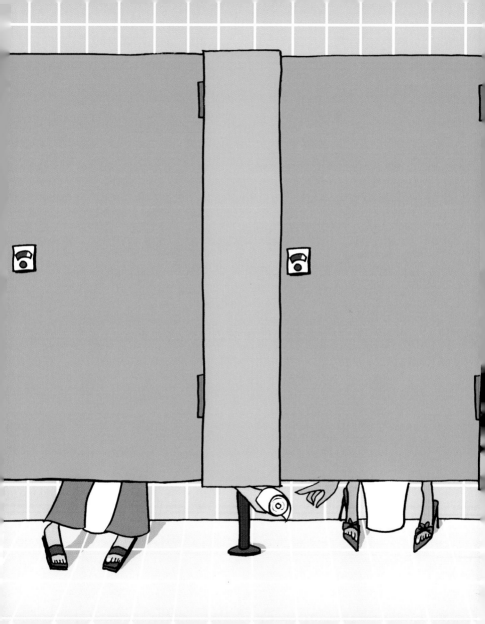

Having someone to keep you motivated

Someone to share your most
valuable possessions with

Someone who's always
there to back you up

Someone to window shop with

Someone to hold your hand
when things get rough

Having a partner in crime

Someone who really knows you

Someone who feels your pain